Bliss of Bewilderment

Birgit Bunzel

Proverse Hong Kong

2017

Supported by

Hong Kong Arts Development Council fully supports freedom of artistic expression. The views and opinions expressed in this project do not represent the stand of the Council.

Bliss of Bewilderment is Dr Birgit Bunzel's second collection of poetry.

Birgit Bunzel was born and raised in Oberhausen, an industrial city in the Ruhr Valley. She left Germany in the 1980s, and has since lived in Taiwan, China, America, and now in Hong Kong. She teaches Chinese and Comparative Literary Studies at the City University of Hong Kong. She won the International Proverse Prize for Poetry in 2012 for her first collection *Shadows in Deferment,* which contains poetry marked by frequent moves and many travels, and by inscriptions from different places, cultures, and people. This second collection turns her encounters into spiritual journeys that begin in bewilderment and end in bliss. Birgit Bunzel has previously published poems in *Mad Poets Review, Clockwise Cat, Kavya Bharati, Cerebration, International Literary Quarterly, Asian Cha, Lakeview International Journal of Literature and Arts,* and, among others, in *Poetry Against Terror: A Tribute to the Victims of Terrorism.* Besides writing, she likes painting, reading, and photography.

BLISS OF BEWILDERMENT

Birgit Bunzel

Proverse Hong Kong

Bliss of Bewilderment
by Birgit Bunzel.
Alternate edition published in paperback in Hong Kong
by Proverse Hong Kong, April 2017.
Copyright © Proverse Hong Kong, April 2017.
ISBN: 978-988-8228-80-5
Available from https://www.createspace.com/6948992

1st edition published in paperback in Hong Kong
by Proverse Hong Kong, 27 April 2017.
Copyright © Proverse Hong Kong, 27 April 2017.
ISBN: 978-988-8228-79-9

Distribution and other enquiries to:
Proverse Hong Kong, P.O. Box 259, Tung Chung Post Office,
Tung Chung, Lantau Island, NT, Hong Kong SAR, China.
Email: proverse@netvigator.com;
Web: www.proversepublishing.com

The right of Birgit Bunzel to be identified
as the author of this work
has been asserted by her in accordance with
the Copyright, Designs and Patents Act 1988.

Cover image and design by Maja K Bunzel Linder.
Colour images by Birgit Bunzel.

All rights reserved. No part of this publication may be reproduced, stored in a retrieval system, or transmitted, in any form or by any means, electronic, mechanical, photocopying, recording or otherwise, without the prior written permission of the publisher or publisher and author. The book is sold subject to the condition that it shall not, by way of trade or otherwise, be lent, re-sold, hired out or otherwise circulated without the author's prior written consent in any form of binding or cover other than that in which it is published and without a similar condition including this condition being imposed on the subsequent owner or purchaser. Please contact Proverse Hong Kong (acting as agent for the author) in writing, to request any and all permissions (including but not restricted to republishing, inclusion in anthologies, translation, reading, performance and use as set pieces in examinations and festivals).

British Library Cataloguing in Publication Data
A catalogue record is available from the British Library

Previous publication acknowledgements

Bunzel Linder, Birgit. 2016. "european winter shoes", "Two Friends". *Lakeview International Journal of Literature and Arts*. Vol. 4.1 (February): 37-8.

_____. 2015. "On the train." In Fabrizio Frosini (Ed.), *Poetry against terror: a tribute to the victims of terrorism*. Amazon Kindle e-book.

For in the dew of little things
the heart finds its morning
and feels refreshed.

                    Khalil Gibran

Sell your cleverness and buy bewilderment.

                    Rumi, Masnavi i Man'avi

To the one whose inspiration always surrounds me.

Bliss of Bewilderment

Contents

Author's Introduction		15
I BEWILDERMENT		17

Bewilderment 21
Yarmouk Camp 22
Seeking Refuge 23
The Captain 24
Lonely Like Rilke 25
On the Train 26
Spring Revolutions 27
A Visit to Your Bazaar 29
Paper Love 31
Breathing in Venice 32
Shakespeare Unloved 34
A Bird Built a Nest 35
stone diaries 36
Saratoga County 37
The Law 38
Coming Home 39
Sorrow 40
Dislikeable Rhymes 41
Ice Flowers of Dismay 42
Letting Go Like Rain 43
Lion of the Heart 44
Claws That Till the Vineyard 45
Best Friends from Cradle to Grave 46
Singing for You 47
As Though 48
a rose is a rose 49
Opa and Oma 50
Unfinished, Like a Ghost 52

Two Friends	53
Near and Far	54
the quiet before the storm	55
Your Anger	57

II   SEASONS   59

At the End of Your Season	61
An Autumn Tree	62
the old pear tree	63
The Zodiac of My Life	64
Desert Rose	65
Courtyard of Peace	66
Mother's Grave	67
Rita	68
Lost	69
Sightseeing	70
Deep Silence	71
Winter Suicides	72
Shadows of a Long Day	73
Change in Weather	74
Practising Death	75
Warning (Un)Hoisted	76
I Miss Winter	77

III   FAITH   79

Dusk Chorus	81
european winter shoes	82
The Placelessness of the Beloved	83
It Broke	84
Throwing Stones	85
Prayer—A Foreign Language	86
The Old Bird	87
Your Name	88
a quiet voice	89
In a Cage	90

Faith	91
On the Lofty Mountain of Life	92
La dolce vita	93
Sea Shells	94
Night Prayers	96
a voice	97
White Fire of Surrender	98
Between Two Shifting Shores	99
Turmoil	101
what lies within	102
Willow Doubts	103
flint of hope	104
I Have Made You My Tenderness	105
IV SUDDEN STIRRINGS	107
At Lucy's	109
The Cat that Sat Next to Me	110
an evening walk	111
The Old Poets Have Said It All	112
Cloudy with a Chance of Poetry	113
It Takes a Long Dark Night	116
Loneliness	117
A Ghost Gets off the Bus	118
On the Way to the Supermarket in Beijing	119
To Ann Arbor	120
Still Tired	121
We Built a House	122
In a Flash	123
V DEW OF LITTLE THINGS	125
The Crickets Inside of Us	127
What Was Said to the Rose	128
East Sees West	129
Dew of Little Things	130
The Unwinged Sparrow	131

Farewell to a Son	133
no entitlements	134

VI   BLISS   139

Bliss of Bewilderment	141
Bliss	142
in the breath of God	143
all night long	144
just a summer day	145
after the monsoon	146
Eggs à la Williams	147
Like the Wind	148
Ignorance is Bliss	149
The Fall of the Moon	150
Saturday Love Soup	151
Moon Ruffles	152
Let Me Be	153
Fear of Falling	154
Prince on a Social Pea	155
Birch and Grass	156
A Perfect Match	157
Freedom	158
You Follow Grief	159
love	160
But Still I Can Sing	161
the final rose	162

ILLUSTRATIONS

Searching	19
Finding	163

Author's Introduction

Bliss of Bewilderment is a collection of poetry that depicts inner journeys I have taken many times. The poems span several years, and it is through this retrospective look that I see my recurrent path: from bewilderment to bliss.

Bewilderment is neither chaos nor storm. It is neither unhappiness nor fear. Bewilderment is a solitary look into questions, mysteries, loss, and facing the unexpected and the unknown. Sometimes it is just coming to an end and not knowing the next step. And very often it is the realization that things are not in our control anymore or simply need to remain unresolved. It could be sweet confusion and it is almost always a surprise. Rumi once wrote, "Cleverness is mere opinion, bewilderment intuition". So, if we practice listening to our bewilderment inside, it ultimately leads to more expansive understanding, a greater acceptance of the "givenness" of life, and a clarity of heart.

This clarity of heart is the foundation of bliss. Bliss is neither loud, nor public. Bliss is what fills the heart when there is a sudden solution, a final thought, a new perception, divine providence, and especially the realization of love and of forgiveness. It is a quiet yet brilliant light that calls back into life, energy, trust, faith, and into humanity.

Sometimes the path from bewilderment to bliss lies in the recognition of changing seasons and growing faith; other times, it is in the joy one can find in little things, the sudden stirrings that can light up the soul. Bliss is the joy that builds a home in the heart, and helps us, "live along some distant day into the answer." (Rilke)

Perhaps to some, bliss and bewilderment seem like unreconcilable opposites. Here also I agree with Rumi who wrote, "God turns you from one feeling to another and teaches by means of opposites, so that you will have two wings to fly, not one."

Birgit Bunzel
Hong Kong, February 2017

References

Rumi, Jalaluddin. (2002 repr.). *Masnavi I Ma'navi: The Spiritual Couplets of Mauláno Jalálu-'d-Dín Muhammad Rúmí* (1898). Trans. by Edward Henry Whinfield. London: Trubner, p. 191.

Rumi Daylight: A Daybook of Spiritual Guidance (1999), trans. by Camille Adams Helminski and Kabir Helminski. Boston: Shambala, p. 143.

Rilke, Rainer Maria. (2004 repr.). *Letters to a Young Poet*. Trans. by M.D. Herter Norton. New York: Norton. Letter 3, p. 13.

BEWILDERMENT

Searching

Bewilderment

You say, "Pray for bewilderment,"
and I am lost in humanity.
Heaven is crossed,
the earth undercover.
I walk my soul
and soon I stumble.
I unleash my mind
and quickly I err.
My eyes seek a solemn path,
my hands reach for clarity.
Silence brews into a storm,
raises nature alone to paradise.
The moon waits for my gravity.
I collect rocks in my pocket,
just to stay grounded.
But already my heart
is whirling in bewilderment.

Yarmouk Camp

Tears cannot irrigate
parched pavements and parched hearts,
fractured so long ago
into fossilized hope.

Seeking Refuge

Never have we feared spring as much as now.
"A heart that is distant, creates wilderness round it,"
one bad translation says.
Wilderness we don't mind.
It is the blossoms that seem
more piercing than thorns.
We left without a kind return,
to welcome spring in unknown plains.
But springs of the past are still in our hearts,
their petals heavier than rocks.

The Captain

Oh captain, my captain,
you sail the seas with a searching soul.
Your eyes consult the rusty compass,
your fingers trace ancient maps.
And when the storm arises,
you double your effort.
In a gale, your heart gathers
the cries of the circling gulls.
When waves threaten
to swallow the ship,
and sharks smell the nearness of death,
you do not look for the Light
to lead you out of the mist.
But when the seas are calm again
and the ship steers straight ahead,
when the sun sends gentle rays
and the gulls glide in new-found peace,
then your mind begins to wage
its own wars, and wishes for storms,
and for the albatross to lead you out
of the soul that cannot sail.

Lonely Like Rilke

The way it sinks into my soul: slow
like a boat in a water lock.
The way it hovers in my heart: dense
like fog on a freezing lake.
The way it spreads in my brain: frantic
like traffic in this metropolis.
I want to swim.
I want to run.
I want to fly.
But the sadness that has risen
from dark and fearful nights
now rains down on my house
and dampens every room.
I go to sleep and dream
that all is washed away,
down the village paths,
and into gracious river arms.

On the Train

The train glides past autumn fields and withering gardens.
It crosses rivers and highways,
rides past local graveyards, where row after row,
lives rest under engraved marble stones.
"Why think of sadness when it adds nothing to life's span?"
some mystic once wondered.
I close my eyes.
But the rapid rumbling of the rails suddenly turns
into far away wars that advance toward me fast.
The soft swaying of the wagon becomes
the slow sinking of refugee ships.
When the train slows and a nearby car tire blows,
panic strikes in eyes that are weary from bad news.
Terror multiplies to the beat. History repeats itself.
Like a thief it comes, stealing borderline ideologies.
You turned to talebearers of delusion, who said to you,
"Wear belts that are engraved, *Return to Sender*!"
"Go fall in a land of disbelief!"
Nobody knows where to find the field that lies out
beyond ideas of wrong-doing and right-doing anymore.*
I don't know where peace lies.

*Rumi

Spring Revolutions

On a certain spring day at noon, the sky darkened.
The earth slowed in amazement,
the wind changed its direction,
and all the birds fled the Square.

A solitary man walked,
his back still not bent
under the burden of the past,
his eyes sheltered
from the storm of the day.

Behind him, the River
is slowing down,
becomes sluggish,
polluted, finally falling
asleep to the lullaby
of no more revolutions,
no more unknown soldiers,
gunshot holes long pasted over.

And now he lies,
not in a coma, but in a trance.
He dances in his Fata Morgana.
Yet he has a dream…

Of someone kissing the desert sand.
Of an enemy giving him bread and water.
Of police guarding lonesome condolences.
Of a golden tomb, and not alone.

But the birds on the Square squawk:
Peace, peace, where there is no peace!

Let the reddened stones of the Square
loosen one by one.

Let them hurl themselves
at the false giants of the day.
Let them summon back the birds,
the desert larks and goldcrests,
sunbirds and orioles,
desert finches and silverbills,
wagtails, pipits and mistle thrush.

Do not die, Blessed of the Nation!
Do not say good-bye
to the stones of the Square!
Let the birds perch
one by one, each on a reddened stone,
and let them hurl
their gritty good-byes at you!

A Visit to Your Bazaar

You invited me into your bazaar.
You offer colourful goods,
specially chosen for my taste.
You say there are cakes and figs,
there are books and scrolls,
there is fresh water for the summer,
and hot tea for the fall.
You say you'd send everyone away
if I want to be alone.
You say you will sit next to me,
if I need to lean on you.
I was afraid to enter
your shop of miracles and delights.
I had no currency,
no idea what price there would be to pay.
It is all free, you said.
It is for you alone, you said.
But you must come every day, you said,
otherwise others will come.
I did not want to enter with empty hands,
nothing in this world is free,
and especially not this kind of trade.
Most of your shelves were empty.
I dusted them off
and set up my goods.
You locked the door.
We used everything up.
I closed my own shop on the other side of town.
One day I asked,
Where are your goods?
Where are the cakes and the figs?
The water, the tea, the books and scrolls?
You smiled and said,
I am too tired to offer them to you.
I got thirsty and asked for water.

You gave me diluted vinegar.
I got hungry and asked for bread.
You gave me unwashed stones.
I asked you to sit next to me.
You just smiled and turned away.
I asked do you want me to keep your shop?
You said it is already kept by someone else.
Someone else who is also
thirsty and hungry.
Someone else who has paid
for all your goods
with life.
Still you talk about your colourful goods.
But behind your closed doors,
there is emptiness.
And as for me, my shop burned down.
And you stood next to me and never said,
"I am sorry for your loss."

Paper Love

A drop of blood from my heart
fell on the tabula rasa of love,
and it spread and it lingered.
"Look at the shapes", you said,
They are the leaves of my country,
the streets to my home.

A tear from my eyes
fell on the red stained paper,
and it spread and it lingered.
"Look at the shapes," you cried,
They are the brooks near our orchard,
the branches of our olive trees.

When you look up, I see
a faraway land in your eyes.
You smile and you say,
"Everything's alright,"
and when you turn,
you brush the paper to the ground.

Breathing in Venice

Silver shards on the water
drop from majestic palaces.
Red brick, copper towers,
marble pillars, gold mosaics,
illuminated by noon light.
Elegant sea gulls sail
over the water streets,
defiantly low, showing
the silver lining of their white wings,
landing on the coffee table
on St Mark's Plaza.
A guidebook opens to
"What to do in Venice in the rain,"
and I remember a friend who said
"In Venice, weather never matters."

There is no queue at the Henri Rousseau exhibit
near the Laguna,
or at the Gothica glass exhibit nearby.
But when I enter the Academica exhibit,
the museums suddenly are dark.
The churches are dark.
The alleys are dark.
The waterways are dark.
History is dark.
Breathing in Venice is like
inhaling secrets
and exhaling aftermaths.
Resting in Venice is like resting
in someone else's golden cage.

It fetters my feet of freedom
and my hands of faith.
Everything shimmers and outshines
the dust and the shards of history.

Martyrdom and beauty.
Enlightenment and heresies.
A world ruled by men.
What do we search for in the narrow places?
Answers to the same old riddles?
We thank forgetfulness,
we take pictures of all the glory.

We study history to enlighten ourselves,
to become part of another world.
Still stirred by the day, I turn on the news,
and I cannot help but wonder
whether we should not rather have studied
the human heart.

Shakespeare Unloved

Polonius cries from the rooftop.
His laughter seeks no echo to mate.
The cloak of truth thrown to the bellhop.
Voices falter into a silent debate.

The Lady snatches doom's lightning,
but darkness is her soul's domain,
sweet coals of revenge incinerating
whom yellow bile of bitterness enchains.

Edgar dances his bound feet sore,
enticing none, but since you ask:
not in love and not in war,
but in loss we tear the mask.

A Bird Built a Nest

A bird once built a nest
that was too small for me.
So I was first to leave
and learned to fly from bees.
When I returned again,
there was an old cuckoo
in our cardinal nest
and spoke of going south.
So I departed south,
and soon I lost my way.
This is how I arrived
where everybody thinks
that I am a strange bird,
singing a foreign tune.

stone diaries

the rocks that were formed
in my heart,
in and out of season,
were baptized in coping strategies:—
stealing skin,
mending heaven,
cropping silhouettes.
had I looked back sooner,
would I have seen the wayside warriors?
recuperated on chalk milestones?
folded up my shadow and run?
but I have to stay.
on this battlefield,
I am not fighting you;
I am fighting myself
in my own prison.

Saratoga County

Love rushes through my heart
the way the Kayaderosseras river
rushes through the thickets
of this land.
What we long for
is also what we fear.
And we are not
like a well so fresh, but
like the rusty waters
that gather on mountain paths
after the rain.
Yet we rush on
with the reluctant winter geese,
lost in flight.

The Law

The lowered gaze sees nothing.
The heart sees you, far away.
The silenced voice becomes deaf.
You still sing your song alone.
My spirit is tamed from roaming free,
shackled to your clock.

I do not listen to love anymore.
It was sent away with the whispering birds.
The birds came back empty-beaked,
unwilling to sing of hope anymore.

Once we watched the ocean move.
We listened to trees shaking their leaves.
Now we watch time advance,
and we bow our heads toward Peace,
each in our own darkness.
The last smile I see
is always of another,
while the hands that serve you,
do not belong to me.
The heart sees you, far away,
an angel on each side.
I see myself, too:
a black raven on each shoulder.
Everything is according to The Law.
The lowered gaze sees nothing.

Coming Home

I walk through commercial hallways,
and past all the gates into other worlds.
Suddenly, through security,
my heart drops into emptiness.
I follow you, but you are not by my side.
My own return suddenly moved
a mountain onto my heart,
and it sinks and sinks into nowhere,
into bleach, into dust, into lukewarmness,
whitewashing it for the veil of expectations.
You are so happy,
you welcome me back.
But I come from so much farther away than this place.
I come from serenity,
from the nest of a silver dove,
from the cave of the hermit dweller,
from the hillocks of Fragrance.
You open your arms and welcome me back
to a storming sea without anchor,
to shaking trees,
to thorny roses,
your tender arms.
What I have built is too big.
What I have hoped for is too high.
What I have done is too incisive.
And all that happened is too vast.
I am home.
But I am not back.
My soul still trails behind.
Please summon it for me.

Sorrow

Snow feathers its wings toward east,
swans plume above lightning sheets
that slowly sink into deep crimson glow

toward a horizon that is shelved
between a blue metallic dome and
rivers that coil around green hills.

I know there is life below:
not from the dim lights of distant homes,
but from the sorrow in my heart.

Dislikeable Rhymes

The Saturday sun sets slowly
As I spew   alliterations for you.

Such a long time since brown and blue
Have swirled   in border-crossing ado.

From some virtual channel you speak
About the price   of cheese and meat.

Between my anger and your pout
Both wander   lonely without clout.

Upon your return you put down
Your bags   with a frozen frown.

Already when last night's sun set well nigh
I heard birds   change from song to sigh.

The Saturday sun sets slowly
As I spew   dislikeable end rhymes for you.

Ice Flowers of Dismay

Because it rained that night,
you went to your coziest home.
And where was I?

Two people face each other,
voice to voice,
and water runs in between.

It pools around us,
but your hair did not get wet,
and neither did your hands,

as though on that rainy night,
someone had opened the floodgates
for me alone,

and every drop dipped deeper
into my rage, and finally formed
ice flowers of dismay.

It left faint imprints
on the spring window,
which I never cleaned.

Letting Go Like Rain

I live on a sacred hill.
The monsoon urges itself in from the outside.
I read poetry, notes, my open calendar.
How desperate we are for you, rain!
Bring thunder, too!
Between every movement
hovers a ghost of wasted faith past,
of fires to be leashed,
of throats to be soothed.
The rain beats its own beat.
It marches into my stomach.
I melt in the rain.
I swell in the rain.
All the many ways of loving are streaming down from
heaven.
They dance so sprightly on the pavement.
Their breezes just brushed my ear.
I am home, the window next to me open,
and I think of you.
I am not alone, I am not just one raindrop.
I am also a storm,
and I wait to learn this:
letting go like rain.

Lion of the Heart

A sudden wind lifts
half burnt paper ashes
and whirls them into the sea.

I run to catch words, letters, signs,
to save them from drowning,
but the tempest takes them from me.

That he just toyed with the breeze,
and that there is fire left,
my misty eyes did not see.

Thus, tears drop like beads
and douse the gleaming coal
by accidental decree.

The icy cold wind laughs
like a hyena and cries,
"The Lion of the Heart
is tired of his prey."

Claws That Till the Vineyard

When southern breezes brood
over brand new shoots of vine
in the valley of delight,
and the "grace of God" sweeps up
the green-eyed maiden,

When the mirror drops,
and shards caress the blood-red puddle,
and the right hand knows not what the left
had fisted up all along
for the green-eyed maiden,

When plans are made in haste,
like dancing through a minefield,
and silence stiffens an army
of narcissus hanging their heads
for the green-eyed maiden,

When time's ignorant bliss
lets sun and moon grow dim in turn,
and a thousand murky knots inside
turn into wrinkled rivulets
for the green-eyed maiden,

When under the copper moon we gaze
at the bazaar of fresh feelings,
a button lost and the thread still twitching,
a final trickle from a distant glacier,
for the green-eyed maiden,

When sand in the hour glass
turns to stone at 6am,
then we know that claws tilled the vineyard,
and when we reckon the due for our deeds,
nothing adds up.

Best Friends from Cradle to Grave

Dawn sun rises behind windy Northern Woods.
Swirling fragrances surround old stately trees.
Cypress and cinnamon,
fir and fringe,
musk and myrrh,
pair up to conduct cicada choirs.

Time-honoured ghosts of sudden delight dispatch
a messenger of fairy dance in silvery waters:
    a rare warbler
    the colour of milk
    with five drops of royal ink,
blue like the shiny earrings that have dropped
from your cerulean eyes.

We dreamed of flying to the star at Dipper's end
that never shifts in a thousand years.
    Muse of my mishaps.
    High place of my mercy.
    Meridian of my soul.
Thoughts tiptoed ahead to times of frail white hair,
but stumbled into your bed made of soil.

And now, like a lost beast seeking the herd,
I chase memories of diamond doves soaring wing to wing.
    "A pelican of the wilderness.
    An owl of the wasteland.
    A lone bird on the rooftop."
The sun high in the sky inches up on a heart half ajar
in which everything but peace dwells.

Singing for You

As though death in his grave, tired and wounded,
summoned back life to rest by his side,

so our song searches for you with bitter lament,
from darkened depths to the palm of your hand.

Let your soul recline, pay heed to my zither,
it is for you alone we sing so sweet, so bitter.

We sing of eyes that glow with ancient pride,
and of forgotten dreams in the midst of night.

We sing of figures that outnumber the ghosts
that with holy kisses betray unheavenly hosts.

Behold, our songs are sung for uncried tears,
for you alone we sing so bitter, yet without fear.

As Though

The winds veil and unveil,
as though there was something unknown to see.

They draw chalk marks on the blue board,
as though wanting to sell us the sky.

Trees shake lush with leaves,
as though hiding secrets in their branches.

Seagulls drop their cries,
as though shooting recent memories.

A feather drifts by alone,
as though intentional in its ways.

Only the grass stays neatly combed,
standing at attention for the grand finale.

Your eyes inspect the dance of the winds,
as though able to decode their choreography.

a rose is a rose

a rose is a rose, but
when petal after petal is plucked,
what is left are thorns.
i ask you:
is it still a rose?
yes, a rose is a rose,
even after you pulled off my petals
and i only show thorns.
we were good together,
petal and thorn.
we were fragrant and strong,
especially in the rain.
you were soft, i held you tight.
but you let yourself wither, petal after petal,
until all my thorns were exposed.

Oma and Opa

Oma in her heavy black dress
was like a ghost forced
to drop anchor in an alien world.
Opa was but her undefined shadow
whose rare words always cut sharp into our fear.
He brought them from East Prussia to the Ruhrpott.
Catholic, with bacon and onions.
You took us there for kindly visits,
not to show us off,
but to squeeze us into the corner of the couch.
Don't move, don't touch, don't talk.
The sooty ghost dragged through the house on
slippers slurping over the stone floor.
Later, when blood oozed out of her skin,
we were ushered into her sickroom,
even more silent than before.
She lay under thick covers,
a heap of "dobranocs", I whispered.*
The shadow had left her side
and folded himself into his grave.
When she was buried, my black and white checkered dress
was soiled by a pigeon.
Mother cried and wore black mourning attire for six months,
and adopted her shadows.
I did not miss her.
I did not love her.
She was a ghost of Polish onion soups past,
with a son who changed his last name under Hitler.
But Opa did not allow them to run
with the delirious masses.
I am child of but one of their ten children.
I can tell a lot about her.

But ghosts don't like to know
the darkness of other people,
the shadows of their decisions,
and the grief of their fathers' sins.
When she died, her dark anchor
sank into my mother's heart,
and as if by default, it then it sank into mine.
Daughter, when I die,
don't stand too close to me.
Don't let my darkness drop into you!

* "good nights" in Polish

Unfinished, Like a Ghost

In our city, billboards are flags
that crowd in the wind of redundancy.
A new wine shop opened, its doors
framed with crockery birds,
put one more sign in the way of the wind.
You say, don't bring candles, they cry.
Flowing flowers shoot flames.
They grow arms, hands, fingers,
red, yellow, blue, violet, pink, purple and grey,
out-picassoing Picasso in our city,
branding walls with tainted riddles,
such as, "What are your twenty-four truths today?"
Then we toast to the moon, once again,
who quilts the streets with seamless shadows,
until the first tasting is done.
Spirits rise on wings,
carry us to where
the cleaver of the daybreak
cuts the sun until it bleeds.
Some take it for the wine of one night;
some know that novelty,
in all its glitter and its bliss,
simply means that life remains
unfinished,
unfinished
like a ghost.

Two Friends

Two friends accustomed to solitude
encounter each other for the very first time.
Unyielding looks eased from the ground,
meeting with the incisiveness of the Other,

One with the feverish glow
of the hunted animal,
the other with the arduous intensity
of deepest anchoring.

Under the early morning moon
panic and meekness feel for each other,
born of mother and of earth
in the haunt of tears, sweat, and blood.

One still beholds morning stars
at the transfigured horizon of time.
The other harkens the voices
at the threshold of world and netherworld.

Pale, tired, they ease into high grass,
deep and wide, breathing in and out.
The more profound perception grows,
the more reticent their Beings become.

Now and then, however,
crow and oriole hear
the unencumbered laughter of one
becoming the other's agonizing lament.

And when the early morning moon
quietly bows to the sun's greedy glow,
what to some is reason for grace,
to others becomes guilt alone.

Near and Far

You, father,
never commanded.
You, father,
never expected.
You, father,
never punished.

You, father,
never guided.
You, father,
never inquired.
You, father,
never embraced.

You, father,
only cried once (?).
You, father,
did not want to do such a thing.
You, father,
still never complained.

You, father,
were always near.
But reachable, father,
you never were.

quiet before the storm

the village is quiet before the storm.
the wishing tree sways above the roofs.
the sea changes colours
and sends muffled roars across.
the dark green mountains sway,
howling with the wind.
and here and there laundry flutters
horizontally in the wind,
though heavy with rain.
clouds merge and move
above an air lacking birds.
only one finch sits on an antenna,
oblivious to the eye of the storm.
the surrounding mountains bow in sorrow,
knowing that they can't shelter us.
here and there a leaf descends.
a bee flies by without looking at me.
joss paper flashes red and gold.
from the graveyard far away,
there are frantic heron cries,
and a lonely dog barks.
i look out to the sea and wait
for the ghosts to rush at me,
to sweep me off my feet.
but the storm rises from behind,
pushes through the plenty trees.
i stand with my coffee
on my rooftop and wait.
i owe it to you to know the coming of change
when you fall silent.
i should have known
that it was not that you found peace.

i watched the storm arise.
i saw it eye to eye.
and i ducked for shelter
and then
could not find you again.

Your Anger

The mountains stand arrogant in their repose,
their trees become prophets of silence.
The ocean is its own master,
its rain glosses over everything.
Your anger is coming in waves
and turns me into a pilgrim again.

SEASONS

At the End of Your Season

When you were gone,
spring fern did not uncoil,
a summer tree fell off its roots,
autumn was unwilling to fall,
pregnant clouds swallowed snow.

Roots abandoned the soil.
The forest exiled its habitats.
A red leaf fell on wet asphalt.
A flake blew lonely across arid land.

Whatever time has woven into law,
time has yet unraveled.
Whatever law has decreed for time,
time saw yet fit to mend.
Perhaps whatever fell out of season,
may yet live on eternal, too.

An Autumn Tree

In my youth,
wild leaves fell off the tree,
even when I did not sway.
I wanted to hold on,
but gravity pulled them
down into the soil
that was nourished by
springs to come.
In old age,
soil has given a new tree.
Sometimes I, too, swayed,
grew roots of wisdom
under bark of pain,
until in the evergreen end,
I, too, withered into truth.

the old pear tree

the autumn wind blows
through the old pear tree.
some leaves swing wildly,
some hit a black branch.
the ones that are golden
fall prey to fall first.
the ones that are green
are ripening still.
some seek comfort in the moment,
others seek solace in change.
some pick the perfect pear,
others gather the fallen fruits.
the tree just knows to let go.
and when the autumn wind blows
through the old pear tree,
its branches bow in gratitude
until it tenderly unfolds again
after the first spring rain.

The Zodiac of My Life

The moon in matchless grace
all but waits to draw you near.
Subtle shadows silently call,
silv'ry dust caresses your face.

Slowly, slowly you call the tide.
Gently, gently you draw me near.
Always swaying between here and there
and the movements of life, now and then.

I have sent turtles into the sea,
inscribed messages on their shells.
Forging my fate by way of words,
I am waiting for their return.

The news they brought back was brief:
there is a time for everything under heaven.
Between the tides of possibilities,
the zodiac of our lives
might form in our firm intents.

Desert Rose

In a soot-black night desert winds howl.
Eerie branches withstand them with might,
but leaves twirl in fading defiance.
This morning will ache under the yellow soil.

Suddenly I remember you
standing in the bleak courtyard that day,
violent fear in your black eyes,
no courage to wave, neither you nor I.

Darkness, wind, and abandonment,
infrangible storms of nature,
but our feelings are like insects:
buzz, without solace, fish feed the very next day.

I was afraid of drifting away,
on a path back, covered with sand.
"We all come from somewhere,
Desert Rose," you once said,

"Do not wither, ever."
But now I listen to the wind from below,
watch you, lost as you are.
Rose-thorn-anger in desert wind,
still waiting as ever
to fade into peace.

Courtyard of Peace

They picked their spots before their curfew.
The things they had to do to get there:
birth, completely;
play, sometimes;
school, for a few years;
and then some more
work, forevermore.

One scuffled through Weimar times;
one through East Prussian fields;
nine siblings here, nine siblings there,
beef stew and sausage for meals.

The war crushed his leg,
and it crushed her heart.
He detoured through
Russia and France,
she through husband
One and Two.

Together at last,
with an offspring of nine,
they went to pick their spots.
They tried to get there sooner:
he with beer, cigarettes, trauma;
she with gloom, qualms, cancer.

In the end, she beat him to it,
and she got first dips.
Every Saturday since, he went
to envy her for her repose,
until in the seventh year,
he fell off his chair
and was finally sent to share
her courtyard of peace.

Mother's Grave

You made your bed under chestnut turf,
same humble landing as kings and serfs,
summoned with multitudes to the paradise tree,
but you alone leave a void in me.

In unfaltering trust, you lie in your grave,
while I still have my path to pave.
Am I a player in your heavenly dream,
or are the children you have never seen?

Saint Joseph's has a weathercock on top,
its pointed crest jolts a hole in the cloud.
You were to me what mist is to rain,
your passions not from a common spring.

When you were mortal and with breath,
you filled your gardens with bitter cress.
No one was willing to understand
the riddles you wrote into the backyard sand.

Soon, oh, too soon you were taken abroad,
hopefully ushered in with long deserved laud.
Throughout my life, you have been my muse,
now not like mist to rain, but like morning to dew.

Rita

Pale is your face and your skin so thin,
like his soul, like your soul.
Your gaze cannot decide
between question and rage.
Perforce.
As so often in life.
Finality is the lead actor.
You say they have eaten away at you.
Thus the cat also meowed.
Grey eyes move like search lights.
They cannot set anchor.
Without you,
I am not myself.
Without your skin, your face, your soul,
your questions, your anger.
Perforce.
Like on our first morning in the Southern City.
What have we learned since then?
That tears are named Secret?
Who has bent the soul and suffocated it?
Who has avoided facing judgment?
Two orphaned birds, unwilling to migrate.
Yet I am the one who asks:
Now that you have crossed alone,
do you have clarity for both of us?

Lost

I walk out on my constant memories,
like a weary soldier leaving the land.

I let go of what is deepest in me,
like deserted platoons splitting at night.

I break my engagement with the future,
like a helmet dropped into trenches.

I chase my faithful shadows away,
like fickle ashes blown off a burnt map.

I separate myself from my thin skin,
like a hasty border-crossing refugee.

I dance the cyclic routine of the self,
like guards rushing their rounds in winter rain.

I feel drops hurting my skinless flesh,
like salt bullets on open wounds.

I am divorcing myself from myself,
like a battlefield pulling out of war.

Sightseeing

A small crow boat glides
through autumn morning mist,
glides into the ancient cave.
What mystery is there to see?
Scars of sinister storms?
What echo is there to hear?
The silence of the barren plains?
We saw the burgundy tallow tree.
We saw snowy reed flowers.
We saw bats lined up like an army at attention.
We saw a kingfisher dancing alone at the shore.
We saw a red dragonfly suspended in the air.
We saw golden leaves twirl toward the south.
We saw grain softened in the water.
We saw fish seeking fish.
We saw a water bug ballet.
We saw white swallows mirroring themselves.
We saw a silver comb adorning the deep.
Perhaps it sank here after the storm.
What is it that binds us to the deep?
What is it that makes us long for the earth?
Is it the dead that went before us?
At the end of our travels,
we rest our oars.
And we see ourselves in the clear green pool.

Deep Silence

Last night after midnight prayers,
a strange silence settled in me,
a strange quietude,
eternal and secret,
like the unvoiced language
of ghosts and spirits.

Into this dark,
a black swallow came from the south,
whispered into my ear
about all the trouble
angels have taken
to soothe my soul.

Winter Suicides

This Tuesday morning,
I found myself as empty as a shoe,
wedded to a paper doll,
Old Mother Hubbard's child,
not yours.
All of a sudden,
the world is not up for grabs anymore,
and even if you wrapped your soul
in fancy gift wrap,
I could still hear its elegy through the boxed walls.
My dead mother knits with her fingers now.
My dead father's snore rattles my heart.
My dead half-sister just an inkling of the past.
My dead friend still a twitching thread.
Always when the moon rises over their graves,
under a strange spell of transference,
a maple leave sinks
right into my stomach.
Hungry as I am,
I shop for bread
in a country as far away as passion.

Shadows of a Long Day

On the light study table
the golden sun throws shadows,
washed out grey in grey,
ironed flat and crisp,

Tossed across the wooden knots—
shaped like sails that set to sea—
by three upright soldiers
who stand at attention on my beech:

The lip balm that calms
my nervously dry lips,
to use as needed,
and that means: all the time;

The eye drops that relieve
my red and itchy eyes,
to improve my strained vision
four times a day: five at least;

The nasal spray that shoots
puffy air into my obstructions
to improve my breathless sleep
two to three times a night: or more;

My army, my saviours!
Upright among the waves of grain!
I shift your shadows into blunted shapes
with the nighttime lamp: countless times.

Change in Weather

Mountains of stiff whipped cream spread
on glassy blue jelly,
and on top, a perfect slice of sparkling lemon.
When someone cracked the plate,
it fell with a bang,
and then there was only clear soup left,
and in it rock sugar,
and some chocolate mousse
covered with powdered sugar.
Their lord has an eating disorder:
he, too, doesn't live by bread alone.

Practising Death

In autumn we sweep,
like golden sisyphi,
leaves that fall like sleep,
to practice death.

Brown branches
still reach to whip
what the wind has lashed
at noon: November.

We live with a maximum
of illusion. Otherwise, would we
sleep?

The only disturbance
is the call of the cockatoo
at midnight sharp. Why worry,
he cackles, in this tropic terrain?

No leaves fall, hot nights rise.
Death is of an unlikely kind:
The kind of sultriness.
The kind of overdraft.
The kind of whirring fans.

The kind of wrong words.
The kind of lost loyalties.
The kind of homeless shackles.
The kind
of turpentine
tears.
The kind of exile.

I go to sleep and practice death.

Warning (Un)Hoisted

We refuse to bid farewell
to the dawning thunder
that bellows brazenly over the peaks;
to our lightning that cracks and crazes
as crisp as first winter ice;
to voluptuous clouds engorging the sky;
to metallic rain squalling in the streets;
to the gods who send us sticky notes
of nature and their attaché Mr Luke Warm
who reminds us coolly
that everything that begins must end.
They beat their fatalistic drums.
They wash clean the floors of memory.
Those who rule on ordinary days—
limp street lights, compliant trees, roads of servitude—
are brushed away and tarred when the wind
maddens our vagrant moods.
Muddy feet march on blackened streets.
Someone must reckon the dues for all deeds.
But when we see the sun, we are as before:
the ash cloud that covered the land
turns into soot pluming from city chimneys,
and everywhere, the fragrance of flowers
dims our memory.

I Miss Winter

I miss winter when
the cold isolates us.
I miss the touch of the icy mailbox,
the darkness of privacy inside.
I miss being wrapped up alone
in fog and frost.
I miss taking out your warmth
in my winter coat.
I miss releasing it into the world,
to let them know you are alive.
I miss the frost on my cheeks
that suspends my tears
before they drop into the public eye.
I miss people rushing by
toward the steam of morning coffee.
Seldom is there so much seeking.
I miss the clarity of barren trees
and the blackness of leftover birds.
Seldom is there so much precision.
I miss life being muffled
and snow falling muted,
and my traces being whitewashed.
I miss sleep that covers me.
I miss flurries filling the gap of my memory.
And when snow angels visit me,
I miss flying into whirling dreams.

FAITH

Dusk Chorus

The dusk chorus is hushed.
A silent moon cuts into the black of night.
I toss and turn in the chrysalis
that life has delicately spun for me.
At the white breaking of day,
I hear the blackbird intone
the dawn chorus with songs
of battle and of love.
When the sun has flushed out the dark of night,
sparrows finally fall in.
I envy the birds their order
when disarray encloses me.
I watch a host of butterflies
gently caress the air.
My own dormant wings fill
with my dreams and stir
to the tumult of the heart,
as though hope might tremble through.
When a pair of magpies drops
a silver chain of trills,
I pray for it to sound
a simple morning hymn,
not yet a fall lament.

european winter shoes

a fresh white snow shrouds pale and fallow fields
where long ago there lay a no-man's-land.
still here and there, the wind whisks latent leaves
off frozen branches, and frozen berries
sink deep into the future that awaits.
the snow has bleached the old and faded blood
of wars, which unfurled borders and gave in
to lands of boundlessness that sprawl right here.
and when the swelling mist in sudden haste
uplifts, we see the tracks of worn out shoes
that sought our refuge, freezing tears of those
who long have known how soon these tracks that mark
a fear… a hope… a fear… will melt away.

an egret stands white and still in the snow:
let us, too, not be hunted anymore.

The Placelessness of the Beloved

There is a bird over every river,
sometimes sheltered by clouds,
sometimes flying free.
The rivers flow in peace,
and where they gather,
birds gather, too.
This is where you bring your heart,
and it brings in the fish,
and for a moment,
the universe convenes
all of its signs
and mirrors them
in your trembling heart.
From there they rise again:
cyclic flocks of echo birds
that spread across all riverbeds,
far beyond the east and the west.
They shed their feathers in the inner world,
letting go of flight,
letting go of song,
letting go of trees,
perching instead
on the placelessness of the Beloved.

It Broke

Last night it broke,
in the storm and in the rain,
in the mountains and at sea.
It broke steadily,
not like branches falling off the trees,
nor like rockslides off the cliff.
It broke slowly,
not like tiles falling off a roof,
nor like a ship that hit a rock.
It broke naturally,
not like a trunk struck by lightning,
nor like a city swallowed by a tide.
It broke calmly,
not like a window hit by ice,
nor like a volcano's rupturing crust.
It broke silently,
like an abandoned spider web.
Still, it broke suddenly,
like a tumbling house of cards.
Last night it broke,
in the storm and in the rain,
in the mountains and at sea.
What is left are yet unheard songs
that will trail the heart
that breaks into humility.

Throwing Stones

Love walked along the railroad
toward evening's red
until it disappeared.
You walked in the other direction,
and you got off the track.
When it all seemed too far,
you thought you'd take a risk,
but your bag was full of rocks.
By what magic was it that
you did not hurl the stones,
but skipped them all across the lake?
Each stone a confession,
each stone a cry,
each stone a weight of love.
Only one you threw at the burning sun,
but it melted in mid-air.
A wildfire burned your empty bag,
and you walked home
unscathed and light.

Prayer—A Foreign Language

The monkeys of the heart rattle the cage.
Black ravens screech and land
on the moor of lies that has encrusted the soul.
My prayer is like a foreign language.
I can only say the most basic things,
and I don't know if you understand.

Dawn settles on me like a thief,
and mists over my glass slippers.
Deep calls to deep at Mount Mizar.

Fields are quilting the land.
A perennial heart progressively unfolds
like magpies circling the tree
without a branch on which to perch.
The broodings of bitterness as relentless as cicadas.
In a cobweb's time,
we come to a peak just short of heaven.
There is an avalanche of tenderness,
doves of devotion sing.
Flasks of wine are set in pairs,
and you smile in spite of my guilt.
Heaven's charge runs into me.
We join as branch to leaf.

My prayer is like a foreign language to me,
but not to You.

The Old Bird

The old bird on the broken ladder
has watched our house for years
and has sung some secrets to us;

Of the sun who always waits
for us to rise until He lights up
the world for His worship;

Of the moon who always cuts
crooked deals with the sea,
cycling slyly between two poles;

Of the nets that are always cast
to catch an abundance of fish
raised in a haunted lake;

Of the wind that always whistles
hasty calls from jinn to jinn
through the jasmine-weighted air;

And of us who never know
whether it is demon or angel
that visits in our dreams.

Your Name

I do not think of your name—my blood inhales it.

And it flows in billowing waves,
beating your heart to awaken to mine,
making your darkness my soul's cradle,
alluring your every stirring of the mind
to travel on a blood cell of mine.
I call to you from far inside myself,
where you are fulfillment and absence,
where you pray within me and where you unfold,
widening your heart toward heaven
and toward love that cannot be captured,
not by words, not by meditation, even less by desire.

Could it be captured
off my blood,
out of the dark,
off the waves,
and imprisoned in rhymes?
It could also be hunted
and confined.

Don't be reticent, my Love,
like cold winter walls!
But be silent, my Love,
like the root of a tree in fall.

Don't be fickle like the flames
that burn in cypress woods!
But be elusive like a deer
panting for life,
or like a poem
not yet conceived.

I do not think of your name—my blood inhales it.

a quiet voice

under the shelter of the leaves,
beams of sun sieve through the crown.
egrets guide a fisherman to their prey.
the errant sapling that suddenly sprouted last spring
has puffed itself up with ripened foliage
and has become home to swinging birds.
the wind whistles faintly into the autumn air,
yet there is a stillness that has laid itself
across the rocks and gentle waves.
in it a voice speaks quieter still,
like the voice that whispers in prayer,
that contains the world and life and humanity,
but forms no words that can be owned.

In a Cage

Only when the bird first stretched its wings in flight,
did it know that it was in a cage,
that life was not her life
but an observation only.
That she sang along with the songs of the street
did not make her a participant.
That she fed on worms
did not get her invited to the banquet.
But once she flew,
freedom carried her wings.
The dark flitting quiet birds
became leaves.
The other collective birds
became colourful.
Her song became part
of the morning choral.
The world did not come to watch her,
but she woke the world.
Only when the bird stretched its wings in flight,
did I know I was in a cage.

Faith

I talk to seagulls
and they whisper back to me,
faster than the wind above the unbridled sea.
The moon a chalk mark on the dark blue board.
"Look behind you, look back behind you!"

I am walking the life line
along philosophy's shore.
Waves wallow unasked,
and sand breathes unmasked.
The past swells like clouds.

All along the salty sea,
water washes my faithless feet,
washes away the trace of me,
claiming another unguarded heart.
The seagull whispers quietly,
"Look behind you, look!"

I look back and see it swirl:
one autumn leaf still
following me,
perhaps from last year's fall,
or even from the year before.
"Perhaps even," the seagull whispers,
"from cradle to grave."

On the Lofty Mountain of Life

From the East, envy rushes
up the hill like wildfire without
regard for fiend or friend,
disarming nobleness along its way.

From the West, love negotiates
its course through mazes of
second-guesses and desire,
looking back too many times.

From the North, faith scaffolds
through the underbrush, rummaging
in philosophies and doubt,
always attached to its twin, fear.

From the South, knowledge struggles
Upwards, steady on stilts, shouting
a proliferation of discursive possibilities,
attuned prominently to the deaf (yet not mute) Other.

High atop a lofty mountain of life,
commotion topples and turns and never arrives.
Feet not planted firmly
dance in anticipation, hoping for
angels catwalking through this life.

La dolce vita

When I asked for shelter,
You tore down my shack.
When I asked for bread,
You took my clothes.
When I asked for companions,
You gave me leprosy.
When I asked for warmth,
You sent frost, night after night.

Time-honoured ghosts laugh
in the valley of the blue moon,
as I put up picket fences
around what is left of me.

When I asked for faith,
You sent temptation.
When I asked for joy,
You sent despair.
When I asked for peace,
You burdened me with fear.
When I asked for understanding,
I received only shallow replies.

Time-honoured ghosts laugh
in the valley of the blue moon,
as the temple of my mind
searches for comfort and joy.

The high places of my heart
were torn down over time.
As an outcast of life,
You mean everything to me.

Sea Shells

Every wave that tumbles
a shell onto the shore
was wrought out of the deep
that lifts it into form,
dependent on the moon
and on the play of swells,
tossed by impulsive quakes
and speedy meteors,
divided by large ships
and floating iceberg tips,
pierced by a sudden fish,
a sea hawk's preying beak,
and a child's skipping stone.

Seas swell in silent sighs
or roar with fortitude,
are touched by deep debris
and sway in randomness.
They shoal and they refract,
they crest their energy,
inviscid force and flow.
Beneath, deep gravities;
shear powers, up above.
They hurry toward land
and weaken on the shore,
their fingers faintly write
a blue account of deep.

The sea, it sends its signs,
it fills the shell's domain.
It tosses it about,
and back into the dark—
no trace and no recall.
Once, it was occupied
and colonized as well.

But now it makes some room
to house its birthing sphere.
All things are framed with awe
and have their time to reign.
There is as much to lose
as there is to gain.

Night Prayers

Yes, I am waiting to see myself, too.
But, alas, I confess,
the inner mirror is long broken,
and what seeps through the cracks
still only seems to be
a distilled version of my true me.

I go to sleep, I toss and turn
between distrust and dark discern.
The shards rise slowly and unbroken
and burn our sorrows and our ache
that still always seem to be
the coat that long has covered me.

a voice

a voice wooed me
into the desert, and i
mistook it for the voice
of a prophet. the birds
that flew ahead of me,
came back empty-clawed.
the snake that slithered
around my feet went blind.
sand rose into a wild frenzy.
settled onto crescent graves.
with what devotion did you charge me then?
which of my selves did you summon here?

a voice called me
out of the desert, and i
mistook it for the wooing
of a lover. the rain
that fell at night,
fell on others, too.
the snake that slithered
around my feet hissed.
trees dropped into a delirium.
leaves held on like death.
what love did you mandate for me then?
which of my selves did you touch here?

White Fire of Surrender

Another gloomy day,
shrouded in mist. Behind it,
the gods scheme in secrecy
where to drop their fickle favours.
The hustle and bustle of the city
is dampened by drifting clouds
and listless moods.
Those who scurry along
on dutiful pavements
cast doubtful glances at heaven
and its blessings.
They don't know that Prometheus' fire
burns white today,
a white fire of surrender.
In it, we find fate,
we find fortitude,
we find fertile soil.
We burn and cast our lots
with our majestic God,
that ripeness may come to the soul.
He casts it with the heart
that beats so close to me,
that ripeness may come to love.
Sacred illusions rise from the soil,
and yesterday's steps are cleansed
in the tears of silent trees.
There is providence in it all:
doubt, suffering, and joy,
I know not from sacred scriptures
or divination bones,
but from the flicker in the eyes
that shine on a gloomy day,
and spark the lasting fire
that surrenders selflessly.

Between Two Shifting Shores

When I dwelled far and far away
in my Calypso's jealous seas,
I was a stranger in my home,
a hermit between two shifting shores.
I did not think the branches of his life
could suddenly be cut and pruned,
or that his head would rest so soon
toward the blessings of the west.
But I could not rush home, nor hold
the weak'ning hand that once held mine.
I brought gifts and tidings, too.
They kissed my son with tearful pride.
We did not dare to speak the words…
The unimaginable needs
imagination, and finds none,
and so it happens that my dreams
plant voices into my dark night,
that grief has loosed its grip on me
and shrouds my heart in wistful white.
My supplications susurrate
the words of this prodigal child.
They whisper like the summer sand
that drizzles on the window sill.
He smiles and opens his arms wide.
He kisses my forehead with his lips.
He rests his right hand on my arm.
The mirror sees my mother cry:
she still sheds countless tears of joy.
At night, he says, I steal myself
into the corners of your dreams.
I scatter rosebuds there for you.
To you they look like reddened tears.
I leave a clever yellow bird
to nest in our memories.
But you just see my empty chair

and the white gown that houses me.
And then you walk out of your dream,
not paying heed to the *salaam*
that I have laced across your skin.
Think not of me
as brittle under darkened trees.
Think not of me
as lamplight that has spilled its oil.
I come to you, night after night,
I come to tell you yet tonight
the things that you need to be told:
do hear the birds that cross the storm,
and make a place of rest for them!
Do hear the prophets cross the land,
and make a place of peace for them!

Turmoil

I practice dying
and I mourn with a vengeance.
My heart is deaf and constricted,
the needles evenly spread out.
Already the stone is rolled over,
and I lie bravely inside the cave,
a desert lot not even disputed by the gods.
My life is a burden to unbelievers: "Whenever
we see her, we think of turmoil."
My life is a burden to believers: "How does
doubt drop from a ghost?"
As long as there is still a flicker of light,
I listen for feet with good news
and still always hope that angels
will come to rearrange my dreams.

what lies within

we travel to the oasis
to search for shades of green.
with a grey mind
and a tinny heart
we find truce.

upstream they follow the light.

watch the angels, who count our deeds, eat together.
which one profits off our souls?
we have shaved our heads,
we have strangled our hearts.
we are at ease in the dark,
where there is neither male nor female.
everyone remains loveless.
what to feed the black ravens
that wait to pick up the crumbs
off our table of true contrition?
seven times they have circled us,
screeched until the wall crumbled,
feasting on stones long gathered there.

upstream, they follow the Light.

angels rush to pray that we be unscathed,
though the ravens have left us,
unable to fortify
what lies within,
we turn away from the battlefield
and walk upstream.

Willow Doubts

Under a swaying willow tree,
shadows are moving over me.
The sky has parted in dark and bright,
the clouds are covering my sight.

I touch the bark, uneasy at heart,
questions and answers have torn us apart.
The sun is hidden behind leaves of green,
life is like a mystical dream.

Dew has settled on this luscious maze,
a breeze arises and moistens my face.
Answers to the deeper meanings of life
have long escaped my weary strife.

A dragonfly shimmers since days of old,
a tender twig its only hold.
Dainty wings move my listless soul
as I listen to a far-away call.

A wind arises from the meadows nearby,
leaves part and allow me a glimpse of the sky.
Something is there for me to behold,
tidings of wisdom from days of old.

First drops of rain retreat from the clouds,
they meet on the grass and ease my doubts.
Your knowledge is high, too high to attain,
without your guidance I will stumble again.

Under a swaying willow tree,
shadows are moving over me.
The sky has parted in dark and bright,
the clouds are moving towards the light.

flint of hope

the past is now
nearer to me than it was then,
even though the rain
has washed my memories off the wall,
and all the miscalculations
that—after all—
have brought me here.
"don't sit in this darkness,"
you say under the glinting stars.
"follow your stars," I say,
but let me fumble for
this flint of hope i have
that only sparks in the dark
and for a moment will reveal
the keys to paradise.

I Have Made You My Tenderness

"I had a dream of catching
fish from a haunted lake,
their eyes aglow with mysteries."

"I, too, had a dream of being
haunted by a fish, its fins
shiny mirrors dazzling my eyes."

"In my dream, I swam upstream,
but the water thickened,
its bubbles hitting me like rocks."

"I, too, had a dream! Of being caught
in a net, inch by inch, and stones gathering
for my sins, my feet dusty with foreign soil."

When I woke, I sat near a mountain brook,
watching fish fly by, seeing stones
skip with the currents, and someone walks

toward me, carrying a bucket of water
and a white towel, washing my feet, saying,
"I have made you my tenderness!"

SUDDEN STIRRINGS

At Lucy's

We eat fish'n chips at Lucy's,
framed checkered table-cloths,
rattan chairs,
and the Pearl River outside.
You apologize for liking
the colonial style
that warmly reminds you of home,
uncomfortably so.
And you talk about your friends in the shop
whose tragedies have weighed down their lives
into this place.

"We breathe together, share a destiny, heart to heart,"
the PLA announces on the walls
of Shamian Road.

We both sigh,
thinking quietly about
how everything seems to have
its own valid truth.

The Cat that Sat Next to Me

As soon as she sat next to me,
I knew she was a cat.
Her red lips and her thick braid
did not fool me.
I could hear the forest roar
beneath her quiet cotton fur.
And in her eyes,
many nights were lagging behind.
She did not move.
But she was prepared
to jump off the roof
of my many tribulations.
I sent her into rueful streets
to lap the milk of my salvation.

an evening walk

street lights hang mellow
in the dark blue dome.
crickets pierce the air
with crisp cross-prattle.
summer rain glazes
the ironed asphalt,
birthing tardy night-time twins.

shadows cross the street
like guilt-ridden ghosts.

the moon sinks
beneath black water pools,
ruffled into folds
by a skillful breeze.
one more step will wane
the moon into dark.

before you came into my life,
i would have stayed.

The Old Poets Have Said It All

The old poets have said it all:
about history, love, beauty, God, nature.
The new poets echoed:
about breakups, wars, brokenness, technology, madness,
blades of grass.
From every cultural angle,
I sit and read
in the light of the moon,
in the light of the sun,
on the shores of the sea,
and on my balcony.
My heart stirs again and again,
like ripples on the lake.
I traveled across an ocean
of poetic words.
But when I scan the rhythm of my heart,
it still hurts.

Cloudy With A Chance Of Poetry

—Variations on Clouds as Seen from Above—

I
Noon lights in the sky
above grey shadows in grey,
mist like mirrors
moves everything in the wrong direction,
slowly stirring stagnant time.

II
The way clouds paint
a Chinese white glaze
over the calligraphy of tar.

III
Clouds in their stillness laugh
at the roughened sea.
The wind does not treat you
the way it treats me!

IV
You swell with white pride
on your sunny side up.
But below children complain of
your presence in their puddles and pools,
and midday flowers close
their blossoms before their time.

V
Many of the tears that are condensed
in you remain uncried.
They disperse like mute warriors
after their windmill wars,
into a wounded reality,
into bookshelves full of explanations.

VI
Fairies sift clouds and tap on petals
until the hummingbird has had its fill;
until the rose has rinsed its cup;
until the rock has had its tattoo;
until the tree has doused its fingers;
until brushes are filled with clear ink,
rolling down blades of grass;

Until the river breaks the dam;
until mud blankets the house;
until all roads turn to ice;
until sturdy boats have sunk;
until water falls in a rush,
rolling down mountains of debris.

Until all is rained and gone,
fairies clap their wings
to stir up time
that was stagnant in our hearts.

VII

They line up like sheep
and follow the leader
over vast blue pastures.

They are frozen in time
and shift shadows in groups
over rocky grounds.

If one gets lost,
no-one goes out to search
in the ninety-nine heavens above.

There are no wolves,
only large silver birds
cutting them into jet white streams.

And if you hear laughter,
it comes from the stars
who moved far above
this haphazard life,

yet they blink and wink for attention,
night after eternal night.

It Takes a Long Dark Night

It takes a long dark night
to untangle the wool and webbing
of such ghostly thoughts.

A fairy followed him through the maze,
tiptoeing in the shadow,
and feeling what ghosts feel:

Confusion, anger, bewitchment and scorn,
yet a desire to fly and hover
above it all.

They grow wings like feathered sails,
and they wave and shout,
"This way out!"

Ghosts keep their eyes pierced ahead,
looking for sign-posts to
righteousness and punishment.

When their wings tire,
they look for the exit.
When they arrive, their faces are frozen.

After he found his way out,
he took her hand and smiled,
and he pointed to the cozy tea house
to warm them up.

This was just when her wings
had almost withered away.

Loneliness

When you have the soul
of a winter blanket, and
layer upon layer suffocates
under a brimming sky
that drops onto its feet
like a Poukai bird onto frozen moors,*

When icicles like fingers claw
to the hardness of the night,
and hollow boots like hollow angels
gather crystal-clear clichés,
the hunter hunts in open season
and all our questions are swallowed
in his trace.

* The Poukai is a Maori mythological bird so big it can eat humans, and it always lands suddenly.

A Ghost Gets off the Bus

There was a dream:
In a thunderous night
on a city bus, on
the back of the last seat,

Where someone had scribbled:
"I love you" and "I love you, too,"
a magic marker emerged
to erase every trace.

Then,
a ghost getting off the bus,
swirling ashes with every step.
But I, too, didn't look back.

On the Way to the Supermarket in Beijing

I saw the sky in thick yellow-grey, far too early
in the day, and it cupped the air that swelled
with osmanthus, jasmine, and CO_2.

I saw a beggar stacking silver pennies
according to hue, from dark to light
with more devotion than a Kumbun monk.

I saw rows and rows of toothpaste
on shelves, perfectly stacked by taste:
lemon, green tea, jasmine, and bamboo salt.

I saw a man lifting a heavy rock to throw
at a young barefooted thief;
the policeman watched with a stony face.

I saw a lady in tattered jeans and t-shirt
taking her pet pig for a walk on a golden leash,
the pig dressed in a frilly pink dress.

I saw three Lamborghinis waiting in front
of the same traffic light, in the blackest black,
in the poorest district of the city.

I saw a dead gingko tree off the highway, with
one leaf left and an empty bird cage.
When the leaf falls, the cage will be alone.

I saw chalk marks on the street, framing a body
long gone, and the blood turned black.
Perhaps my life is an accident, too?

To Ann Arbor

Misty clouds
draw an uncertain horizon.
Above the skies,
azure blue of eternal peace.
Below the skies,
changing colours,
a kaleidoscope of questions and doubts.
Shadows and shapes shift with the guiding light.
Closeness obstructs the view.
Distance detaches the heart.
Every now and then,
a jet stream of orientation,
a bird, a tree, a wave, a face.
We pass from moment to moment,
collect knowledge and memories
for a collage of life.

Still Tired

My sleep pushed me haltingly
through the night like
through a traffic jam.
The morning tunnel
welcomes me coldly.
The city that spreads in
front of me is
a gray fata morgana.
The sun is trying
to pour her fire colours
over my hair.
I turn around and rush
back into my dream.
But the barriers have
already come down.
I must move forward
and travel the day.

We Built a House

We built a house.
It was too big.
But we filled it anyway.
For a lifetime.
Then a wolf came.
And it was gone with the wind.
And so, a lifetime turned
into a mere journey.
And that was hard.

In a Flash

Today, I looked up from my desk,
and the sun was glaring.
I pulled down the shades.
When I looked up again, the sky was grey.
I pulled up the shades.
I looked up once more,
and the rain and the leaves were hurrying westward.
I turned on the light.
There was no need to look up
for the thunder and the lightning.
Until a sound startled me:
my favorite potted plant had fallen
off the third floor balcony.
I took the broom and went downstairs
to clean up the mess.
This was thirty minutes of Hong Kong weather.

Or was it my life in a flash?

DEW OF LITTLE THINGS

The Crickets Inside of Us

My father left the house
in the early morning hours
with a sigh that was
snapped up by our pet turtle
before it could come to us.
When he returned in the dark,
the turtle stretched out her neck for more.
But he tiptoed by our room quietly,
so as not to wake
the crickets inside of us.

What Was Said to the Rose

The wind wildly shakes
the shrubs and evergreens,
and the blood red rose.
The rain fiercely whips
the houses and the streets,
and the blood red rose.
Lightning sharply splits
the mountains and the seas,
and the blood red rose.
Thunder darkly strikes
the towers and the trees,
and the blood red rose.
Hail firmly lashes
the petals and the leaves
off the blood red rose.
The pilgrim sun still circles
around the yielding world,
and the dark green stem
that now stands proudly armed
with golden sickle thorns,
shields all the words
once whispered to the rose.

East Sees West

Workers from the outskirts
squat for weeds,
stare at the unfathomable entities
passing by from faraway lands.
Their noon hopes are concentrated
on hot dumpling soup.
The only other connection between us
at the ancient Northern Gate
is a stream of white ants
rushing from East to West.

Dew of Little Things

This week I met a man
whose father was a snake-catcher,
and he said, "I followed in his footsteps
and became a process engineer."

This week a hamster died
in my hand and she is still
twitching in my heart, buried now
under copper sand and blue kitchen tiles.

This week I watched her face turn
red and her spirits sink low.
I put chamomile on her face and now
she knows that sometimes I, too, am helpless.

This week I forgot to turn off the coffee maker
in the office and left for another country.
The building burned down in my mind,
and for a few days, I was content.

This week it rained twice when I didn't
expect it, and I realized because nobody
can stop the rain, we have to cope,
just as we should do with our tears.

This week a stranger at the airport
took a photo of me without asking,
and I don't know in which language
I should ask for my soul to return.

The Unwinged Sparrow

I am a tiny sparrow with cut wings
that cannot stir up time anymore.
I perch in the corner behind the glass door
where it is cool and shady,
but counterintuitive;
where mother put me to die in peace.
How else would I have got up those stairs?
Two albatrosses soar by and look down on me.
Their pity adding another shade of cool.
Their heads twitch about my misfortunes.
Unable to fly with such heavy hearts,
the one dressed in gold stretches
his warm claws to pick me up.
The one feathered in white nods
"How it shivers with trepidation!"
"Give it a crumb of bread; give it blades of grass;
give it quickened worms; give it a little more life."
They put me into the dusty grass twice my height.
They let me perch on crusted ground.
They float away, hand in charitable hand.
They take away my hope of mother
coming back for me,
my hope for a merciful death
in the shade, where,
once dead,
I will be found.
They hide me away on no-man's land.
No-bird will look for me.
They leave me to watch the worm
inch by my weakened beak.
They leave me to watch breadcrumbs
twirl in the moonlit wind.
They leave me to die
and be eaten by worms.

They soar away,
hand in charitable hand,
proud to prolong
my solitary death.

Farewell to a Son

Absentmindedly, the heart wrapped
in thorny thoughts,
I clean the living room,
wipe dust off the shelves,
put books back in place,
arrange half-withered flowers,
straighten pillows on the couch,
as though to cleanse my heart
from the debris of time.
I pick up my son's t-shirt,
thrown there casually
when he visited last time
to say his farewells.
I clutch it and it smells
like a detergent I don't know.
I clutch it nevertheless.
It is all I have of him in my house.
I curse the detergent.
He never smelled this good before.
I hope he fares well.

No Entitlements

I
withering of spring
dewy meadows at sunset
my clothes are too loose

II
withering of spring
dewy meadows at sunset
birds feed their nestlings

III
everything withers
my eyes have become dewy
and my clothes too lose

IV
in the summer rain
villages are upside down
contained in one drop

V
a butterfly lands
on the tip of a wet bough
the villages drop

VI
first winter morning:
snow gathers under the door
as white as my hair

VII
a snow owl perches
the moon reflects in the lake
mist rises in between

VIII
after the typhoon
streets are crisscrossed with brushwood
trees stand tall and groomed

IX
in the glow of dawn
on the awakening lake
dragonflies glisten

X
a withered blossom
settles on a spider's web
all is still

XI
early summer day
a red dragonfly hovers
over a lost shoe

XII
a cold winter night
my bare feet step on pinecones
left by my dead son

XIII
after the typhoon
sea gulls float like falling leaves
too soon for autumn

XIV
thunder and first rain
fallowed fields breaking open
insects awaken

XV
the last leaf drifts down
enters the cycle of life
in the swelling soil

XVI
ripe fruits have fallen
empty fields make room again
for the passing wind

XVII
a late summer day
a broken black butterfly
sleeps on the ghost wall

XVIII
under dark green pines
ancient houses lean against
reminiscences

XIX
first spring rain has dried
last year's nests still have feathers
and swallows return

XX
birds sing in choirs
bees settle on open blooms
i wasted my life

XXI
a child faintly cries
muffled by his mother's hug
but my tear still drops

XXII
early april now
all the swallows have returned
but i lost my way

XXIII
on the ripened fruit
autumn is the afterglow
fading into spring

XXIV
beneath the bare trees
the many leaves of summer
wither into truth

XXV
trees sway in the sun
red leaves gather one by one:
laying down their lives

BLISS

Bliss of Bewilderment

We tend to the garden,
find its wilderness
doused in the salmon light
of an Indian summer sun.
Like final autumn leaves,
human beings fall
into each other's lives.
And hopes rise and fall
like gulls, waves, dunes and tunes.
The white river rushes by
all our days of delight:
fast, torrential, into hours of perplexity.
Something grows slow, slow, until
the slow undying of the spring.
We rearrange roots, rocks, blossoms, and birds
to the best of our blindness,
until the dusk chorus sings of
the bliss of our last bewilderment.

Bliss

My thoughts took wing in a raving night,
sorrow and death confined to sheets of soil.
I wanted to send a message of joy to the bird,
but its shade and shadow escaped into the past,
its swift wings beat my wound, my heart.

Our frail white hair like a kiln of ashes
seethes with life lived lodged in one age,
times when the lone beast sought the herd
and eagles cried through layered bends
that let toppling echoes depart.

Once hills and streams made their own clear notes,
and there was no need for harps and flutes.
Fragrances swirled above stately trees,
almost melting the frail first frost
on such silent days of wise complexion.

Now around horses' hooves fallen flowers swirl.
In fields out of season, rooted memories sprout.
But before the valley of lengthened shadows
becomes an industry of thorny thoughts,
sudden lightning summons us back into recurrent bliss.

in the breath of God

white cranes widen their wings
and slowly soar above the water.
a light breeze rises and ruffles the sea.
trees rustle and wake their leaves.

an old man plays a harmonica song
that melts heavy into the sky.
the cranes hover in the plaintive tune,
as though suspended in the breath of God.

only one little egret flutters back and forth,
dives swiftly to snatch a fish below.
he parades his catch, hops from rock to rock,
tiny silver lights blinking from his beak.

when the harmonica falls silent,
the cranes slowly stir and glide back
to the shore where they stand in silence,
as though perching in their souls.

all night long

all night long, your restlessness
paced on the rooftop
near the southern sea,
until at daybreak
worms begin to leaf
through the trees,
waking up the wind:
it began to pace, too.

all night long, your restlessness
ruffled my sheets,
until at dawn,
waves break in the ocean
and spread onto the shore,
lashing the wind
to pick up its pace:
did you feel it, too?

just a summer day

just a summer day by the open window.
the cooing of the neighbour's attic doves
fills the breezes of late gentle june.
the sweet smell of summer milk rises
to the yellow meadow on my wall.
a long quiet novel weaves its dreams
into my lazy days of childhood.
the coal man and the chimney sweeper
are hibernating in their trades
in this bright and early summer glow.

i was aware of the bliss of that moment.
it matured with me until now.
as tough i had known back then
that one day, i will need it again.

after the monsoon

rain falls into rivulets. each
drop filled with a story pushing
down the wind. the swifts
secure their homes.
the wall leans on the ladder.
far away cattle stand crossed
by fences. shadows shrink
back into your skin and darken
your eyes. i lean over to you.
the rain lights up
your hair. i fall
into your gaze and lie down
next to you. finally
run out of words.

Eggs à la Williams

I wrote to you
about putting
all my eggs in one basket.

I told you
about walking
on their shells on tiptoe.

When you said
that he who would have eggs
must endure the cackling of hens,

I suddenly remembered
the eggs
that were boiling
on the stove.

One of them,
in the heat,
had peeled itself completely.

I ate it with
a delightful feeling
of certainty.

Like the Wind

Like the wind, I race
through the cool fresh air.
Like a horse, my thoughts
dash behind me in a trail.
Like a puppy, they charge ahead.
Like a bird, they flutter into the trees.
Like a butterfly, they flitter about.

Like the wind, I race
through the cool fresh air.
And I take leaves with me,
and take flies and bees with me,
and take pollen and take rain.
I pity the snail,
I pity the worm,
I pity the rocks that lie bare.

Like the wind, I race
through the cool fresh air,
I soar, I circle, I swoosh,
until at last I turn to dust
and settle on myself.

Ignorance is Bliss

Ignorance is bliss
   twittered the bird in front
      and flew off in the other direction
         not taking the sun as a cue anymore
            winging it alone like a wood warbler
               heading to the colony in sedentary pursuit
            while the rest of the flock go astray and
         swift and swallow are swiftly swallowed
      by the aimless open sky above
    scattered out of formation so
ignorance becomes bliss

The Fall of the Moon

A god beat his lute so hard,
all the notes fell out of the sky,
and the moon dropped to the earth.
It rolled down the green hill
and bumped this way and that
and finally landed
right in our backyard pool.

Saturday Love Soup

Again and again, I pass the stove
on a late Saturday morning as I rove.
Rain, shine, sun and snow,
your stir is always intently slow,
as though it were a pot of thick paint.

You are exact by vocation
and measured by designation.
The stack of greens impatiently fresh,
potatoes first, then the squash.
We know better than to complain.

Your hands still stained with dirt
from a week full of hard work.
The smell of rust and turpentine linger,
mingling with onion, parsley, and ginger.
The shiny ladle outrules the stumpy brush.

Your call to eat makes us abandon our play.
We rush to the table and solemnly pray.
Eight pairs of sprightly eyes so dear,
ask every Saturday, year after year,
"Daddy, what took you so long?"

"Ah," you say, "there are so many of you.
One ingredient per child or two,
to cook to taste and until done,
with pixie salt and a lucky bun.
Who can rush Saturday Love Soup?"

Moon Ruffles

The boat glides on a calm dark lake.
Cool mist flocks in the air.
The last warbler calls the hour.
Silently, we search the mirror.

Water bugs daintily dent the surface.
A leaf fearfully falls on the water.
A feather with green lashes drifts.
Oily stars drip on rocks below.

A turtle sticks out its old head.
A frog jumps in with a splash.
A wave laps the mossy bank.
A memory drops its rusty anchor.

Suddenly your oar slaps the moon
and ruffles her up.
She convalesces for a few nights
behind a black pirate's patch.

Let Me Be

The sea is partial to the moon,
swaying in its bowl,
the same way I am partial to woe and joy,
hither and fro.
Please, sky, in my next life,
don't let me be walking
in this lukewarm shell!
Let me rather be
a pine on a ridge, silhouetted against
the Blue Mountains;
a dragon fly, flitting
over the rocks of Qinghai Lake;
a Dulin plum, pitted
against a crazy clift;
or a maniac shoot of bamboo.
Sky, oh Sky,
don't let me be this prison
full of barbed thoughts!
But let me be
an owl on a rooftop, roosting
on catchy thoughts of prey;
a frog on the edge of a pond, hankering
for the same princess moon;
a jackfish, frolicking
in the reefs of Bais Bay;
or even a bundled rice sheaf, standing
up proud in the noonday sun.

Fear of Falling

The depth of your eyes in a sea of clarity,
not like burning sun or waxing moon,
but like a cognac diamond dropped on ice.

The softness of your skin and your scent,
not like Irish meadows in tender bloom,
but like sooty soil on sun-soaked prairies.

Your marvelous tone and voice,
not like a brook pitter-pattering in the woods,
but tempered like Fugue no. 2 in June.

The way you walk and read,
not like a scholar under his lonely roof,
but like a shy albatross in ancient air.

The way you listen and reply,
not like father to child in late afternoon,
but like a tilted tree in a drunken forest.

The gentleness of your touch,
neither searching nor acute,
but like a cloud out-hovering the breeze.

The way I want to hold on to you
is like a cage to its bird.
But like rain to mist it should be.

Prince on a Social Pea

There is a thief
on the tacit lose.
First it was just a Bible,
and then it was a believer's heart.
The Great Minister will rebuke him,
sooner or later?
But the Pied Piper calls
down the stars from Hamlin heaven,
his flute alight with *jouissance*.

When you shelter me,
I move mountains.
Far from me,
I only shift sand.
A heavy heart weighs
against three great virtues:
distance, purity, non-interference;
and it weighs my feet
down to an earth
where we rarely walk the road together.

Prince on the social pea,
Stephen Daedalus of the mind,
Hunger Artist of the soul,
all I ask of you is this:
Do not hurt
what is deepest in me!

Birch and Grass
(after Shakespeare's 'The Phoenix and the Turtle')

Hearts remote, yet not asunder;
distance, and no space was seen.
But in them it were a wonder:
so love did shine between.

In me then, thou mayst behold
late grass against its birch retire.
In me then, e'en in twilight's cold
Thou see'st the glowing of such fire.

A Perfect Match

We praise the sun:
fire, light, and glory.
Flowers raise their wings.
Waters offer up a sacrifice.
But the owl
favours the moon:
The great and the little
each has its match:
this is nature.
Today you are the river
and I am the ocean.
Tomorrow we switch:
this is love.

Freedom

Tagore laid his heart redeemed
at his Lover's sacred feet.
In each line he then bestowed
how to tame the wand'ring soul.
It took loss, not verse, to see
the great gap between the free
and the few redeemed by peace.
So we threw our hearts unbound
to a flock of wild black crows.

You Follow Grief

You follow grief like bitterns
follow their far-carrying cries,
restless prayers trailing behind.

Last night I prayed that your soul
may dive into the kind of wonder
the petrel dives into every day,

Suddenly making silence possible,
the same silence with which flowers
weave their skills into blossoms.

May you become a white petrel,
a lone wondrous diver.
May I become a white blossom,
a lone prayer flag.

love

your silence speaks
between the lines
where you hang your heart
next to your soul.
a gust of wind
tosses and turns them
and then
they fall into me
where I have no words.

But Still I Can Sing

So much rain,
and the bird's cage has shrunk.
But still I can sing!
So much sun,
and the water dried out.
But still I can sing!
In the early storm,
the lock split open.
But still I can sing.
A Hand takes the bird
that cannot fly.
But still I can sing.
Lays it to rest
in the field of resolve.
But still I can sing.
It becomes a flute
carved by the Hand,
to play when I sing.

the final rose

words are drawn by the white thread of morning.
words are sketched by the dark thread of night.

birds that slept in your heart left in time.
the wind has come to hunt your straying gulls.

rain drops lines from heaven to earth.
untold stories evaporate in the fields.

in the streets, water walks barefoot.
it buries lamps in its deep solitude.

words fall into the water of your soul—and bloom:
in my barren land you are the final rose.*

*Pablo Neruda

Finding

SOME POETRY AND POETRY COLLECTIONS
Published by Proverse Hong Kong

Astra and Sebastian, by L.W. Illsley. 2011.

Bliss of Bewilderment, by Birgit Bunzel Linder. 2017.

Chasing light, by Patricia Glinton Meicholas. 2013.

China suite and other poems, by Gillian Bickley. 2009.

For the record and other poems of Hong Kong,
by Gillian Bickley. 2003.

Frida Kahlo's cry and other poems,
by Laura Solomon. 2015.

Home, away, elsewhere, by Vaughan Rapatahana. 2011.

Immortelle and bhandaaraa poems,
by Lelawattee Manoo-Rahming. 2011.

In vitro, by Laura Solomon. 2nd ed. 2014.

Irreverent poems for pretentious people,
by Henrik Hoeg. 2016.

Mingled voices: the international Proverse Poetry Prize anthology 2016,
edited by Gillian and Verner Bickley. 2017.

Moving house and other poems from Hong Kong,
by Gillian Bickley. 2005.

Of leaves & ashes, by Patty Ho. 2016.

Of symbols misused, by Mary-Jane Newton. 2011.

Over the Years: Selected Collected Poems, 1972-2015,
    by Gillian Bickley. 2017.

Painting the borrowed house: poems,
    by Kate Rogers. 2008.

Perceptions, by Gillian Bickley. 2012.

Rain on the pacific coast, by Elbert Siu Ping Lee. 2013.

refrain, by Jason S. Polley. 2010.

Shadow play, by James Norcliffe. 2012.

Shadows in deferment, by Birgit Bunzel Linder. 2013.

Shifting sands, by Deepa Vanjani. 2016.

Sightings: a collection of poetry, with an essay, 'communicating poems',
by Gillian Bickley. 2007.

Smoked pearl: poems of Hong Kong and beyond,
    by Akin Jeje (Akinsola Olufemi Jeje). 2010.

The layers between (essays and poems),
    by Celia Claase. 2015.

Unlocking, by Mary-Jane Newton. March 2014.

Wonder, lust & itchy feet, by Sally Dellow. 2011.

THE INTERNATIONAL PROVERSE POETRY PRIZE
(SINGLE POEMS)

An annual international poetry prize (for single poems) was established in 2016. The international Proverse Poetry Prize (single poems) is open to all who are at least eighteen years old whatever their residence, nationality or citizenship.

Single poems, submitted in English, are invited on (a) <u>any subject or theme, chosen by the writer</u> OR (b) <u>on a subject or theme selected by the organizers each year.</u>

Poems may be in any form, style or genre. Each poem should be no more than 30 lines.

Entries should previously be unpublished in any way (except in the case of unpublished translations into English of the entrant's own work already published in another language, providing the entrant holds the copyright).

In 2016, cash prizes were offered as follows:
1st prize; USD100.00; 2nd prize: USD45.00;
3rd prizes (up to four winners): USD20.00.

KEY DATES FOR THE PROVERSE POETRY PRIZE IN 2017 ONWARDS
(subject to confirmation and/or change)

Receipt of entered work, entry forms and entry fees	7 May to 30 June of the year of entry
Announcement of Winners	Before April of the year following the year of entry
Cash Awards Made	At the same time as publication of the winning poems (whether in the Proverse newsletter or website, or in an anthology)
Publication of an anthology of winning and other selected entries	Contingent on the quality of entries in any year

The above information is for guidance only.
More information, updated from time to time, is available from the Proverse website: proversepublishing.com

FIND OUT MORE ABOUT OUR AUTHORS,
BOOKS, EVENTS AND LITERARY PRIZES

Visit our website: http://www.proversepublishing.com

Visit our distributor's website: <www.chineseupress.com>

Follow us on Twitter
Follow news and conversation: twitter.com/Proversebooks>
OR
Copy and paste the following to your browser window and follow the instructions: https://twitter.com/#!/ProverseBooks

"Like" us on www.facebook.com/ProversePress

Request our free E-Newsletter
Send your request to info@proversepublishing.com.

Availability
Most titles are available in Hong Kong and world-wide from our Hong Kong based Distributor, The Chinese University of Hong Kong Press, The Chinese University of Hong Kong, Shatin, NT, Hong Kong SAR, China.
Email: cup-bus@cuhk.edu.hk
Website: <www.chineseupress.com>.

All titles are available from Proverse Hong Kong, http://www.proversepublishing.com
and the Proverse Hong Kong UK-based Distributor.

Stock-holding retailers
Hong Kong (Growhouse, Bookazine)
Singapore (Select Books),
Canada (Elizabeth Campbell Books),
Andorra (Llibreria La Puça, La Llibreria).

Orders from bookshops in the UK and elsewhere.

Ebooks
Many of our titles are available also as Ebooks.